EUCHARIST

Explained by

SAINT PADRE PIO

MARIE-JOSÉE THIBAULT

Saint Padre Pio Speaks - Book 2:
The Eucharist Explained

Published by Abba Books LLC
abbabooksllc@gmail.com
Copyright © 2024 Marie-Josée Thibault

First Edition, 2024
Designed and Edited by Abba Books LLC
ISBN: 978-1-7377418-8-6

Abba Books LLC
34972 Newark Blvd, #441
Newark, CA 94560
www.abbamyfatheriloveyou.com
https://www.facebook.com/AbbaILoveYouBooks/

Thy Peace
on Earth
must be
achieved.
No light,
no litany
must be
spared to
honor Thy
Grace.
-Saint Paul

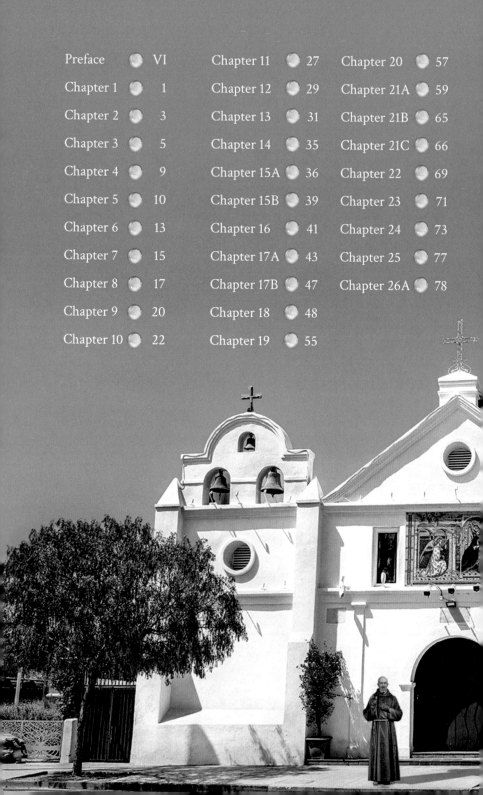

Our Lady Queen of Angels
Catholic Church in Los Angeles
California, United States

Preface

The brilliance of Saint Padre Pio is found not just in his mercy but in his deep understanding of the mysteries of the Eucharist. I invite you to explore this book with an open heart and in unity with Jesus, the Virgin Mary, and Pio himself.

Pio, I love you,

Marie-Josée

Chapter 1

The Eucharist, my children, is the very life of Paradise, the very life of eternity, and the very life of the Kingdom of God, which is given to you under the simple facade of the bread and wine consecrated by a priest and which become the Body and Blood, Soul, and Divinity of our Lord Jesus through the intermediary of the Holy Spirit— God the Holy Spirit. In this book, I will describe the miraculous process that takes place before your eyes and especially in your heart.

I love you. Blessed is he who presents himself at the sacred banquet of the Lamb in a state of meditation and love. Amen. Alleluia!

Chapter 2

The Eucharist, my darlings, is filled with a dazzling divine light from beyond that you cannot imagine—although your heart sees it clearly. Visualize a ball of fire as vast as the sun descending lovingly toward a black cavern with no signs of life. This fire is the majesty and power of the Eucharist given to you during the celebration of every Catholic Mass on Earth. What charity! What a miracle! There is so much love!

I love you. Blessed is he who kneels with reverence and admiration before the grandeur and generosity contained in the Eucharist. Amen. Alleluia!

Chapter 3

The Eucharist, my friends, my loves, is more fantastic than all your wildest dreams, more wonderful than all the rejoicings on Earth combined, and more transformative than all the sermons communicated by priests in their churches. The Eucharist is the most important supernatural event that takes place on Earth at any time and in any place.

Blessed is he who believes in my word—the word of Saint Padre Pio. I love you.

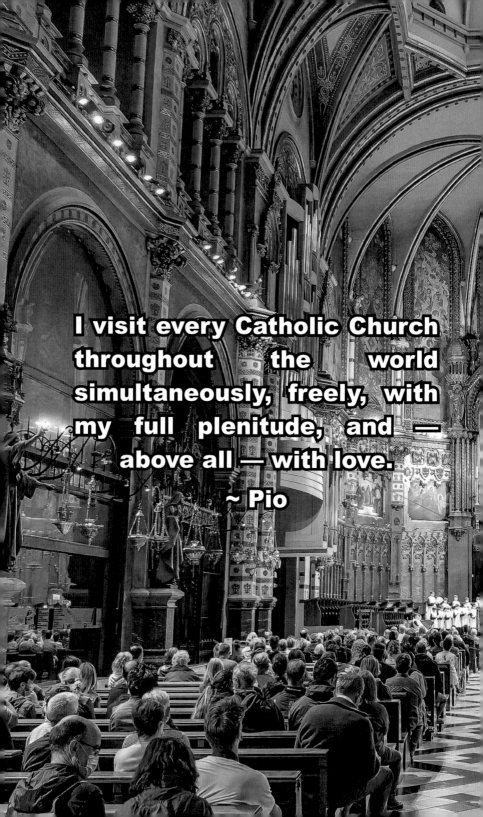

I visit every Catholic Church throughout the world simultaneously, freely, with my full plenitude, and — above all — with love.

~ Pio

Sunny exterior view of the St Joseph's Catholic Church at Wyoming

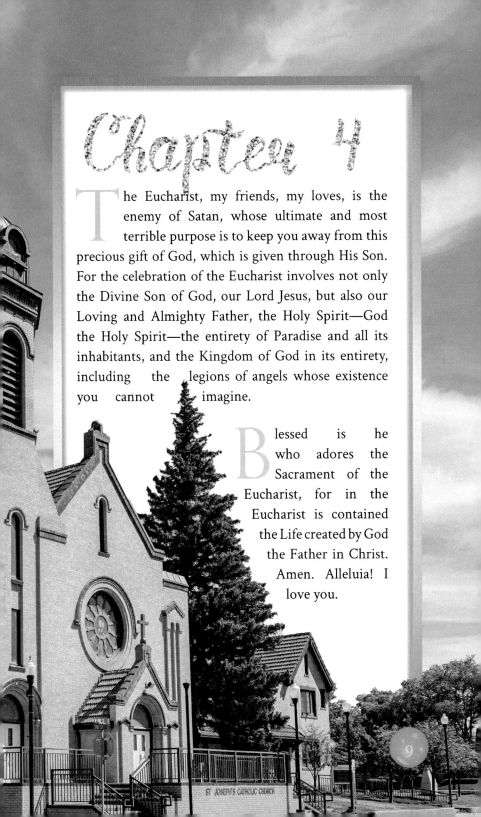

Chapter 4

The Eucharist, my friends, my loves, is the enemy of Satan, whose ultimate and most terrible purpose is to keep you away from this precious gift of God, which is given through His Son. For the celebration of the Eucharist involves not only the Divine Son of God, our Lord Jesus, but also our Loving and Almighty Father, the Holy Spirit—God the Holy Spirit—the entirety of Paradise and all its inhabitants, and the Kingdom of God in its entirety, including the legions of angels whose existence you cannot imagine.

Blessed is he who adores the Sacrament of the Eucharist, for in the Eucharist is contained the Life created by God the Father in Christ. Amen. Alleluia! I love you.

ST JOSEPH'S CATHOLIC CHURCH

Chapter 5

My children, the Eucharist marks the true beginning of your life. In other words, you are spiritually dead until the precise moment in which you receive the sacrament of the Eucharist. Therefore, receive frequently this , Life in Jesus Christ, our Savior and our God, who loves us so much. I love you.

Blessed is he who receives the Eucharist regularly and with great reverence and gratitude. Amen. Alleluia!

Chapter 6

My friends, my loves, God the Almighty Father gave me the order to speak to you about the Holy Eucharist. God greatly desires your transformation and sanctification. As far as we, the inhabitants of Paradise, are concerned, few things on Earth are of any interest whatsoever apart from the salvation of your souls. This is why I speak to you today about the greatest mystery that takes place on Earth: the mystery of the Eucharist—a mystery of love, light, life, and redemption. I love you.

Blessed are those invited to the sacrifice of the Eucharist, to the sacrifice of the Mass, to the sacrifice of Jesus, to the sacrifice of the Lamb of God. Amen. Alleluia!

Chapter 4

My friends in the Holy Spirit, I love you. Today, I will explain to you the very nature of the Eucharist. Through its deep and mysterious nature, the Eucharist opens the doors to Paradise. In addition, the Eucharist is an energetic conduit that directly connects you, who lives on Earth, to Heaven. The Eucharist, my friends, my loves, transports you to the foot of Jesus on the cross in its veritable, cosmic, and transcendent plenitude. The Eucharist contains the past, present and future of the entire Creation, which was designed by Him, for Him, and in Him, our Lord Jesus Christ. The Eucharist, my loves, is the very Life of Jesus. Amen. Alleluia!

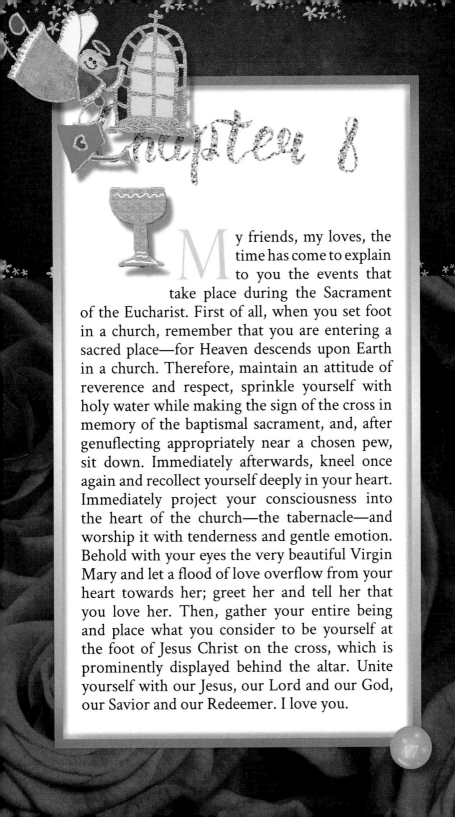

Chapter 8

My friends, my loves, the time has come to explain to you the events that take place during the Sacrament of the Eucharist. First of all, when you set foot in a church, remember that you are entering a sacred place—for Heaven descends upon Earth in a church. Therefore, maintain an attitude of reverence and respect, sprinkle yourself with holy water while making the sign of the cross in memory of the baptismal sacrament, and, after genuflecting appropriately near a chosen pew, sit down. Immediately afterwards, kneel once again and recollect yourself deeply in your heart. Immediately project your consciousness into the heart of the church—the tabernacle—and worship it with tenderness and gentle emotion. Behold with your eyes the very beautiful Virgin Mary and let a flood of love overflow from your heart towards her; greet her and tell her that you love her. Then, gather your entire being and place what you consider to be yourself at the foot of Jesus Christ on the cross, which is prominently displayed behind the altar. Unite yourself with our Jesus, our Lord and our God, our Savior and our Redeemer. I love you.

Chapter 9

My friends, my loves, listen to me carefully. At the beginning of mass, remain in deep recollection at the foot of the cross with Jesus and under the gentle and loving gaze of the Most Holy Virgin Mary. My children, at the beginning of Mass, all of Heaven is engaged in the intense preparations necessary for the Eucharistic liturgy. By virtue of the divine glory that is the tabernacle, the entire Heaven dwells in each church all times, and the inhabitants of Paradise can walk there as they wish. In fact, the ceilings and walls of churches no longer exist, because all of Heaven has descended on it and has touched the floor of the church. This is true for every Catholic church throughout the world at all times, day and night, with or without the parishioners and clergy who serve in the church regularly.

Blessed are the pure hearts who visit and venerate their parish church—a holy and heavenly place without parallel on Earth. Amen. Alleluia!

St. Mary's Mission Church near Maxstone, SK

Chapter 10

My friends, my loves, prostrate yourself immediately before God the Father, God the Son and God the Holy Spirit, the glorious Trinity, who has inexhaustibly given you the infinite merits of Jesus which are necessary for the divine redemption of your soul by virtue of the grandiose and heavenly miracle of the Eucharist. Amen. Alleluia!

I receive with great joy and anticipation each parishioner who enters the House of the Lord — everywhere in the world and at any time.
~ Pio

Chapter 11

My friends, my loves, listen to me carefully. The time has come to explain to you the role of angels during the liturgy. Angels, my friends, my loves, are far more numerous, powerful, and radiant with divine grace than you can imagine. Angels are instruments of the Divine Law who carry out the commands of God the Father Almighty with the same degree of perfection as they carry out the operations of the Holy Spirit and assist in the continuing mission of Jesus on Earth.

The Angels, my darlings, fill every Catholic church to its capacity! Their magnificent wings adorn all of a church's interior space in a unique and graceful celestial spectacle that escapes the human eye but not the eyes of the pure heart. I love you. Amen! Alleluia!

Chapter 12

My friends, my loves, listen to me carefully. I have succeeded in teaching you the essential foundations of the Eucharist through the extraordinary operations of the Holy Spirit, for the Holy Spirit is at work in this book, which has been blessed by God and made holy by the grace of our marvelous Jesus, redeemer of the world. Amen. Alleluia!

Chapter 13

My friends, my loves, listen to me carefully. When you are in church and participating in the celebration of the sacrifice of the Mass, invest your heart, soul, and even body in the liturgy itself. Imagine that Jesus Himself and all the inhabitants of Paradise are brought together out of love for you alone—this is indeed the truth. Jesus, my child, is there in the Most Blessed Sacrament, and He carries in Him the entirety of Creation, whether visible of invisible. I love you. Amen. Alleluia!

Front of Metropolitan Cathedral building of the Assumption of Mary at Mexico City

Chapter 14

My friends, my loves, listen to me carefully. Today, more than any other day in your life, open your heart to the sublime truth that is the descent of Jesus Christ our Lord from the depths of Heaven to the depths of your heart at the sacred moment of the Eucharistic liturgy. I love you. I ✝ am Saint Padre Pio, and I love you! Amen. Alleluia!

Chapter 15A

My friends, my loves, I love you. Listen to me carefully. The time has come to speak to you specifically about the cosmic unfolding that occurs in the Eucharistic liturgy.

When a priest prepares to begin this liturgy, he recites in a low voice a universal prayer known only to the clergy. At this moment, the adoring angels and the executing angels of the Eucharist quietly descend from the heights of Heaven to the altar in front of the celebrant. Heaven is always open and floating freely in every church around the world. The angels and the inhabitants of Paradise move freely in the churches, from top to bottom and from bottom to top; the ceilings and walls of the church are abolished, and the entire Paradise is placed on its floor.

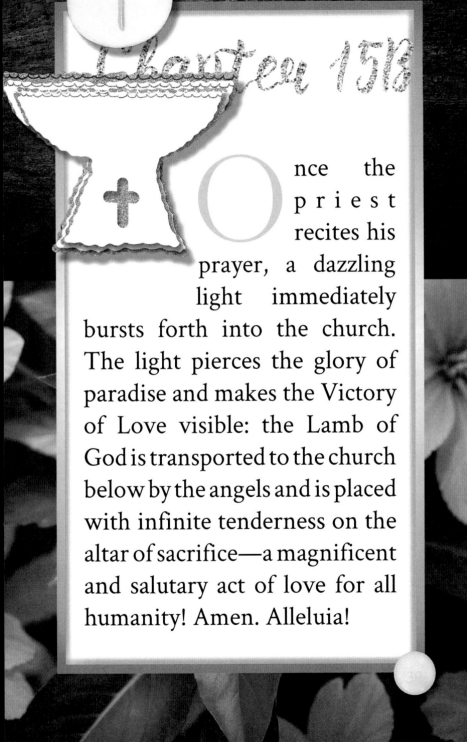

Once the priest recites his prayer, a dazzling light immediately bursts forth into the church. The light pierces the glory of paradise and makes the Victory of Love visible: the Lamb of God is transported to the church below by the angels and is placed with infinite tenderness on the altar of sacrifice—a magnificent and salutary act of love for all humanity! Amen. Alleluia!

Chapter 16

My friends, my loves, listen to me carefully. Today, we continue our study of the Eucharist.

The Lamb of God, as you know very well, is Jesus Himself, our Savior and our God. The Lamb is not a symbol of God or a representation of Jesus or His biblical title. The Lamb of God is Jesus, His body, His blood, His soul, and His divinity, in all His ineffable Power and all dimensions of the cosmos that are known and unknown to man. The Lamb of God, the Redeemer Lamb of All Creation, is Jesus, the same Jesus begotten of God, Who walked the Earth 2,000 years ago, Who is with us until the end of time, and Who will soon return in unimaginable Glory. I love you. I am Saint Padre Pio, and I love you! Amen. Alleluia!

Chapter 17A

My friends, my loves, I love you. Now is the time to speak to you about the Lamb of God, who was transported from the depths of Heaven to the altar of the Catholic Church.

The Lamb of God is Jesus Christ our Lord Himself. This beautiful white Lamb, pure, gentle, without spot and without sin, will lose His life minutes after He is presented at the altar. This beautiful Lamb, which is all white and all virtuous, initially stands on the altar and then kneels before it, His head to the left of the celebrant, waiting obediently and lovingly for the moment of noble sacrifice.

Chapter 143

This triumphant sacrifice, my dear ones, is carried out by the liturgical executor angels at the precise moment commanded by God the Father, which corresponds to the precise instant of the epiclesis, as proclaimed by the celebrant of the Mass—the invocation of the Holy Spirit over bread and wine in the Eucharistic prayer of the Catholic Church.

I love you.

Chapter 18

My friends, my loves, listen to me carefully. I love you! I am in Heaven, and I love you! Thanks to the merciful designs of God, I am able to speak to you and communicate to you my teachings regarding the beautiful, great, and magnificent mystery of the Eucharist! I am Saint Padre Pio, and I love you! Amen. Alleluia!

I love you,
~ Pio

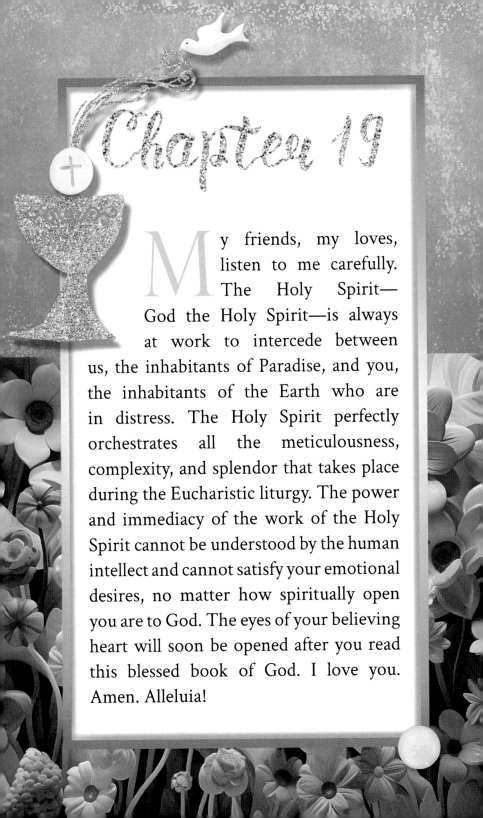

Chapter 19

My friends, my loves, listen to me carefully. The Holy Spirit—God the Holy Spirit—is always at work to intercede between us, the inhabitants of Paradise, and you, the inhabitants of the Earth who are in distress. The Holy Spirit perfectly orchestrates all the meticulousness, complexity, and splendor that takes place during the Eucharistic liturgy. The power and immediacy of the work of the Holy Spirit cannot be understood by the human intellect and cannot satisfy your emotional desires, no matter how spiritually open you are to God. The eyes of your believing heart will soon be opened after you read this blessed book of God. I love you. Amen. Alleluia!

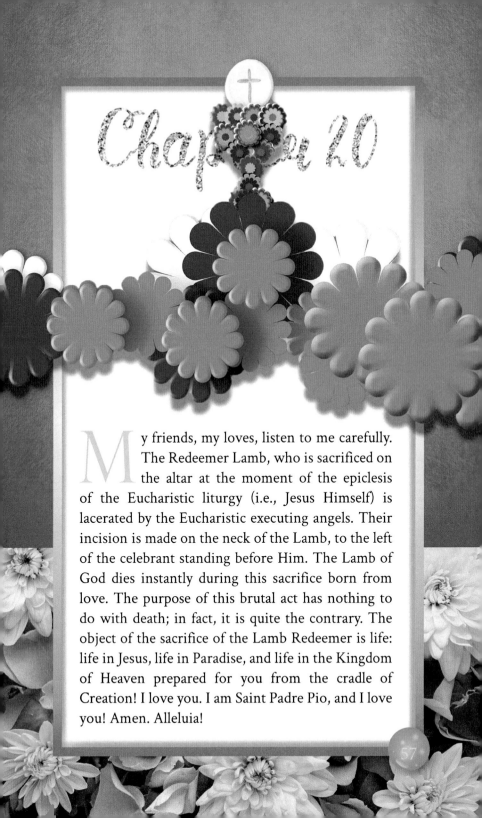

Chapter 20

M y friends, my loves, listen to me carefully. The Redeemer Lamb, who is sacrificed on the altar at the moment of the epiclesis of the Eucharistic liturgy (i.e., Jesus Himself) is lacerated by the Eucharistic executing angels. Their incision is made on the neck of the Lamb, to the left of the celebrant standing before Him. The Lamb of God dies instantly during this sacrifice born from love. The purpose of this brutal act has nothing to do with death; in fact, it is quite the contrary. The object of the sacrifice of the Lamb Redeemer is life: life in Jesus, life in Paradise, and life in the Kingdom of Heaven prepared for you from the cradle of Creation! I love you. I am Saint Padre Pio, and I love you! Amen. Alleluia!

Chapter 21A

My friends, my loves, listen to me carefully. As explained, the sacrifice of the Lamb of God—that is, the sacrifice of our wonderful Jesus—gives us Life. By what means? The eyes of the heart, my darlings, can see the unexpected miracle that unfolds at the moment of epiclesis.

Beautiful Catholic Church Sanctuary of Mary Magdalena in Novelda in Spain

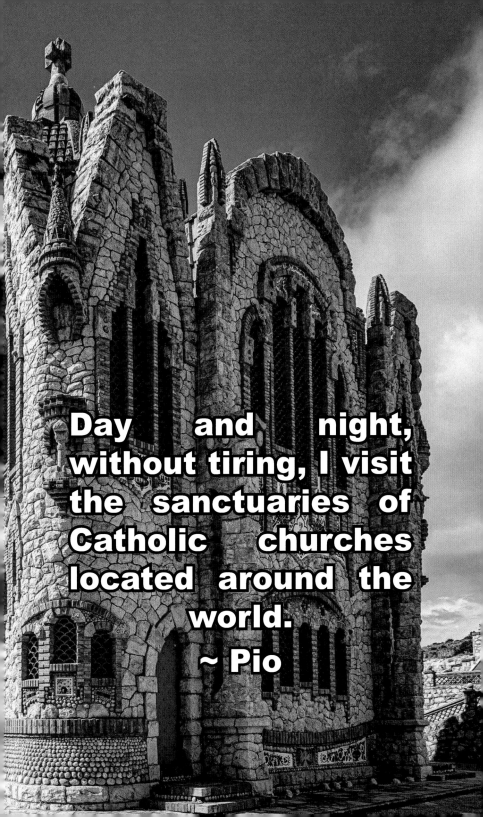

Day and night, without tiring, I visit the sanctuaries of Catholic churches located around the world.

~ Pio

Chapter 218

My children, listen to me carefully. The incision made in the neck of the Lamb causes an immense ocean of blood and water to suddenly gush from the neck of this adorable little animal and flood the congregation with a gigantic supernatural wave that spreads over everyone present, whether they are near or far from the altar, in inexplicable abundance. The entire congregation is washed and submerged by the merciful blood and water that spurts from the neck of our magnificent, gentle, pure, and spotless little Lamb. This unimaginable sacrifice born from love cannot be accomplished without the mystical death and tragedy of the sacrificial Lamb: our sweet Jesus. Do you see?

Chapter 21C

What exquisite Love! What boundless charity! What cosmic mercy! What soothing solicitude from the Father, the Son, and the Holy Spirit! What an ineffable and delicious gift that is Life! Amen. Alleluia!

Chapter 22

My friends, my loves, listen to me carefully. Nothing is more important in your life than adhering to your Catholic faith and regularly living out the prayers and devotions required by our holy religion. Eucharistic adoration and the Eucharistic liturgy are at the pinnacle of the rituals and sacraments of the Church which inspire, purify, protect, transform, and sanctify the souls of believers. So, do not hesitate to submit to God through Jesus, who is present in the consecrated host and wine. I love you.

Chapter 23

My friends, my loves, listen to me with all of your attention. Your heart is much bigger than you can imagine, for the Kingdom of God is within you (Luke 17:21) in your heart! Therefore, your heart is much bigger than your physical body suggests, much bigger than the electromagnetic field that surrounds you, much bigger than the city you inhabit, much bigger than the entire Earth that carries you, much bigger than this galaxy that encloses you, and much bigger than the universe as estimated by astrophysicists!

Your heart is the seat of your soul, and your soul simultaneously dwells both in your physical heart and comfortably in Paradise with us! The part of your soul that is in your physical heart is called the human soul, while the part of the soul that dwells with us in Paradise is called the divine soul. This is why the Bible states that the Kingdom of God is within you! I love you. I am Saint Padre Pio, and I love you!

Chapter 24

My friends, my loves, listen to me carefully. Beyond the worries and vicissitudes of this world exists a radiant, glorious, and magnificent world of peace, beauty, and happiness. This is the Paradise that awaits you at the goal of your life's journey if you persevere in faith in Jesus Christ, Son of God, our Savior and our Redeemer, our All. I love you. Amen. Alleluia!

Chapter 25

My friends, my loves, listen to me carefully. The time has come for me to speak to you about Jesus, who is on the cross during the Eucharistic liturgy.

Jesus Christ, our Lord and our God, is always present in all tabernacles nestled in the heart of all Catholic churches throughout the entire world. How is this possible? I invite you to join me as we explore this highest and most sublime mystery of our religion.

I am Saint Padre Pio, and I love

Myeongdong Cathedral Jung-gu, Seoul, South Korea.

Chapter 26A

My friends, my loves, listen to me carefully. Jesus Christ, our Lord and our Savior, is indeed present in the tabernacle of each Catholic church—He fuses with each Eucharistic liturgy in an extraordinary way.

Jesus, my darlings, inhabits all dimensions of the cosmos, whether known or unknown to men, at all times and with an ineffable fullness. The marvelous sculpture of Jesus on the cross suspended over the altar that you revere in church is part of a continuum of Christ's Energy that envelops the entire Earth and that materializes in varying degrees in different places.

Bless
our
Home

O God, You gave Saint Pio of Pietrelcina,
capuchin priest the great privilege of participating
in a unique way in the passion of Your Son,
grant me through his intercession the grace of ....
which I ardently desire;
and above all grant me the grace
of living in conformity with the death of Jesus,
to arrive at the glory of the resurrection.

Chapter 263

In other words, the cosmic Christ Energy of Jesus is found in its plenitude, that is, in a complete, indivisible, and eternal way through each sacred object devoted to his Holy Name. Our good and sweet Jesus on the cross is truly and delicately present wherever his Glory shines on Earth: every figurine, statue, sculpture, small or large crucifix, painting, mural, drawing, or work of art, including the vibrations of an edifying Christian musical composition!

Glory to God in the highest and peace on Earth to those who love him! Amen. Alleluia!

Chapter 27

My friends, my loves, listen to me carefully. Christ Jesus our Lord is truly present in the tabernacle and in the consecrated host and wine. His body, blood, soul, and divinity are present by way of transubstantiation. The presence of Christ our Savior is found in full plenitude in every sacred object dedicated to His Holy Name, as explained earlier; however, He is present in a more mystical and extraordinary way in the tabernacle and in the consecrated host and wine. I love you. I am Saint Padre Pio, and I love you!

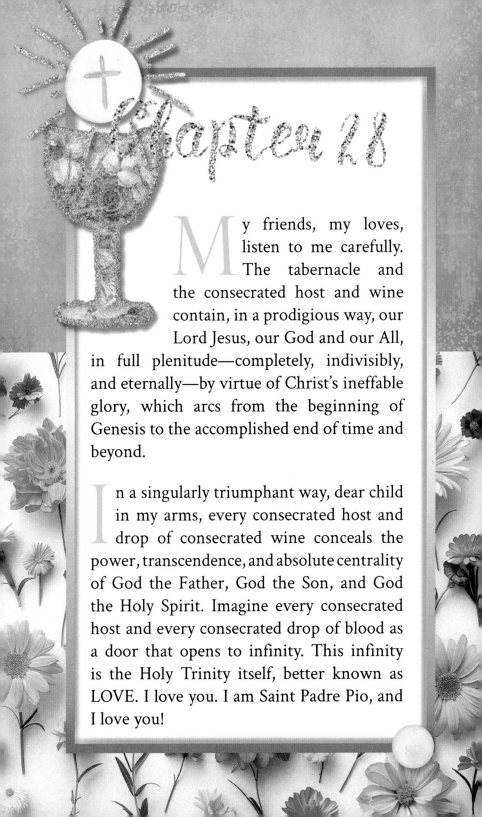

Chapter 28

My friends, my loves, listen to me carefully. The tabernacle and the consecrated host and wine contain, in a prodigious way, our Lord Jesus, our God and our All, in full plenitude—completely, indivisibly, and eternally—by virtue of Christ's ineffable glory, which arcs from the beginning of Genesis to the accomplished end of time and beyond.

In a singularly triumphant way, dear child in my arms, every consecrated host and drop of consecrated wine conceals the power, transcendence, and absolute centrality of God the Father, God the Son, and God the Holy Spirit. Imagine every consecrated host and every consecrated drop of blood as a door that opens to infinity. This infinity is the Holy Trinity itself, better known as LOVE. I love you. I am Saint Padre Pio, and I love you!

Chapter 29

My friends, my loves, listen to me seriously. Much greater is the mystery of the Most Holy Communion! As explained before, the Lamb of God—our Lord Jesus Christ himself—is lovingly lowered by the Eucharistic angels to the altar of cosmic sacrifice. At the same time, by virtue of the operations of the Holy Spirit, Jesus on the cross also descends from the heights of Heaven to the altar of cosmic sacrifice. How is this possible? Imagine a continuum of inexhaustible love the operates on all planes of the universe known and unknown to men, which allows Jesus to live his mission using his body, blood, soul, and divinity he wishes.

I love you! I am Saint Padre Pio, and I love you!

Chapter 30

My friends, my loves of love, listen to me carefully. Jesus Christ, our Lord on the cross, is present in the consecrated host and the consecrated wine. The mystery is thus revealed: our Lord descends from the Heart of the Father our God bathed in a glorious light brighter than the sun. His eternal glory pierces Paradise itself, which remains permanently laid on the floor of every Catholic church. Jesus, our God, is always accompanied by Eucharistic, adoring angels. These Angels, resplendent in their beauty and purity, revere, honor, and adore Love-God made Love-Man for the redemption of all humanity. Demonstrating great virtuosity, angels facilitate and coordinate the glorious entry of Jesus into the low and heavy dimensions where humans live and breathe; stated more precisely, Jesus moves towards the sanctuary of the Catholic church where the celebrant of Mass stands in front of the altar of the sacrifice of love. I love you. Amen. Alleluia!

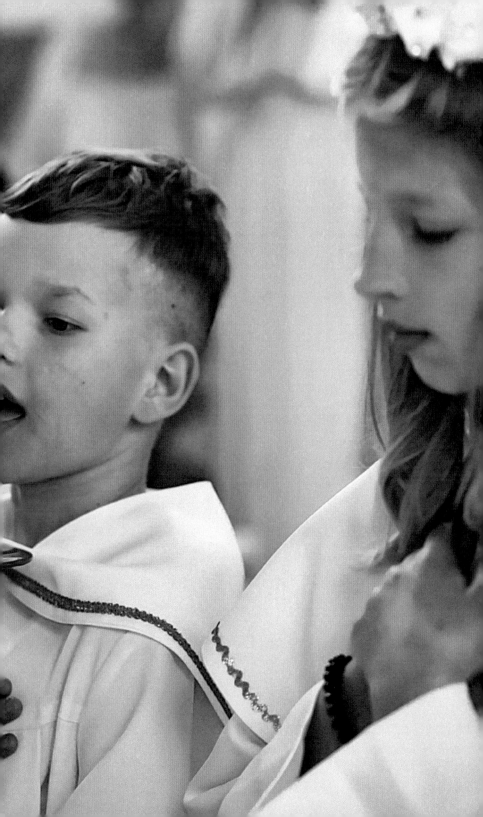

Chapter 31

My friends, my loves, listen to me carefully. The planets and galaxies of the universe glorify God in ways you cannot imagine. The animal, plant, and mineral kingdoms of planet Earth praise God in ways both large and small. Humans, unfortunately, utter only a few words of reverence toward God, our Creator and our Judge. Let us immediately fix this injustice done to the Most Holy Trinity by reciting the Lord's Prayer from the depths of our hearts and with me, Saint Padre Pio:

Our Father, who is in heaven

Hallowed be your name,

Let your kingdom come,

Your will be done on Earth as it is in heaven.
Give us today our daily bread.

Forgive us our trespasses,

Just as we also forgive those who have offended us.

And do not let us enter into temptation,

But deliver us from Evil.

Amen.

Chapter 32

My friends, my loves, listen to me carefully. Now is the time to explain the modalities of transubstantiation. As explained before, our sweet Jesus on the cross is transported precisely and delicately from the highest point in Heaven to the sanctuary of the Catholic church, gradually from above to below. Our Beloved Jesus is suspended in the air and gradually approaches the celebrant during the liturgical Eucharistic prayer, somewhat behind and above. You do not know this, but Jesus our love still experiences agony in His Easter Passion. He once again suffers the excruciating pain, unspeakable bitterness, and true anxiety of his imminent death on the cross. The cosmic tragedy of our God unfolds in every Eucharistic liturgy taking place in every Catholic church, in each and every hour, throughout the entire world. This has been true since Passion on the cross 2,000 years ago and will remain true until the end of the known world. O infinite charity! O inconceivable sacrifice! O sublime divine love! I love you. I am Saint Padre Pio, and I love you!

Chapter 33

My friends, my adored loves, listen to me carefully. Life as you live—it has nothing to do with life, that is, life in Jesus, our Lord and our God. Life in Jesus is life in Paradise for eternity with us, the inhabitants of Paradise, including the angels of God, the Most Holy and Most Beautiful Virgin Mary, mother of all creatures of creation, and Jesus Most High, master of all. I love you. I am Saint Padre Pio, and I love you!

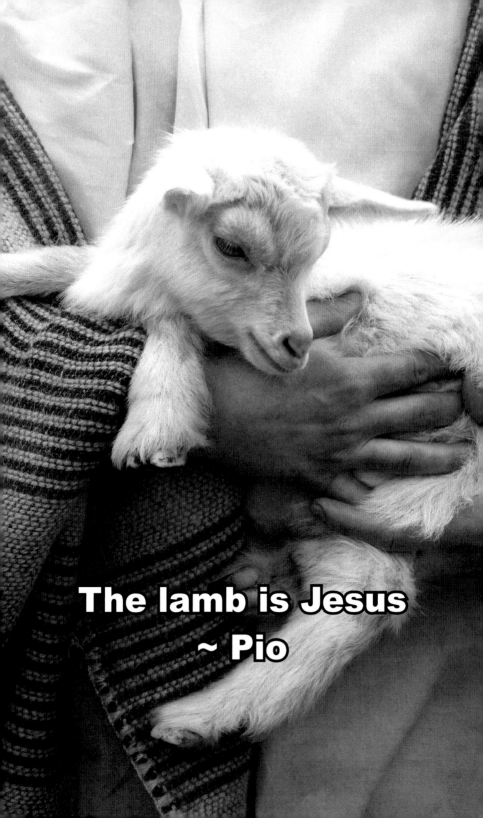

The lamb is Jesus
~ Pio

Chapter 34

My friends, my loves, let us resume our study of the Eucharistic liturgy. God made man, our sweet Jesus, lovingly descends towards the celebrant of the Mass, an ordained priest of the Catholic religion, with the precious help of the adoring Angels and the Eucharistic executing Angels. Jesus's death is imminent with each celebration of his august sacrifice. How is this possible? My friends, my loves in my arms, listen to me carefully. Jesus our King approaches the celebrant from a little ways back and behind; gradually, Jesus gradually moves forward until he merges with the priest—this all takes place carefully and piously. What is being fused? What is this unheard-of mystical phenomenon? We will continue the unveiling of this beautiful mystery shortly. I love you. I am Saint Padre Pio, and I love you!

Chapter 35A

My friends, my loves, listen to me carefully. The mystery of the fusion between Christ Jesus and his Catholic priests is much greater than you can imagine. Jesus must die at every celebration of the Eucharistic liturgy. Jesus our Lord possesses His resurrected physical body; as you know, this is the same body He possessed 2,000 years ago when He walked in the land of Israel. His physical heart still beats with a normal, human heartbeat. This heart is the seat of His human soul, His divine soul, and His soul glorified in the Spirit. The physical heart of Jesus, my child, fuses for a very brief moment with the physical heart of the celebrating priest so that Jesus can die within his priest. Do you see?

Abandoned churches are filled to capacity with Angels.

~ Pio

Beautiful stained glass window in an old church

Chapter 35B

This is why the Eucharistic miracles recorded historically (e.g., Lanciano in eight-century Italy): they demonstrate that the consecrated host becomes human heart tissue—that of Jesus—and that consecrated wine becomes human blood (specifically that of Jesus). Glory to God in the highest, and peace on Earth to those who love Him!

Chapter 36

My friends, my loves, listen to me carefully. Life without Jesus and without the Eucharist is not life, but death in the Spirit. Life, as announced by the Good News of Jesus, is life in Jesus. When Jesus said, "I am the Way, and the Truth, and the Life," (John 14:16) He was clearly teaching others about Life in Him, our Lord and our God, our Joy and our All. I love you. I am Saint Padre Pio, and I love you!

Chapter 37

My friends, my loves, listen to me carefully. Life in Jesus, life in Paradise with us, the inhabitants of Paradise, including the saints around me who adore you and who pray for you constantly, is much greater than life on Earth! Continue reading the books dictated to Marie-Josée T., the essence of Saint Paul on Earth, because these books reveal the truth. They are permitted by God the Almighty Father to accelerate the sanctification of your soul! I love you. I am Saint Padre Pio, and I love you!

View of the basilica of
Lourdes, France

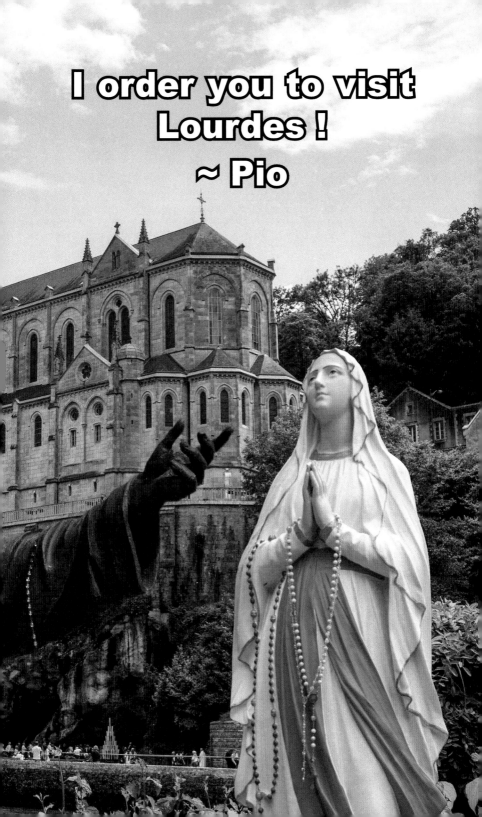

I order you to visit Lourdes !
~ Pio

Chapter 38

My friends, my loves, listen to me carefully. Be vigilant about the educational materials you read or listen to. Satan aims to make you fall and leave our holy Catholic religion by using the elements of your personality (called ego) that are weakened by social scandal, the decadence of the bourgeoisie, and falsely idealized corruption. Avoid anything proclaiming to be an expeditious and universal solution to all your problems, such as drugs or occult practices providing unexplored sensations, as these are nothing other than sacrilegious distortions, well as the absurd promises of ultra-modern instant pleasures, for in these lie the real danger for the soul. I love you.

Chapter 39

My friends, my loves in my arms, I love you. Let us continue our study of the Eucharistic liturgy. Remember that Jesus on the cross, our sweet Lord, lovingly descends towards his celebrating priest at every Eucharistic liturgy in order to die therein through the fusion of the physical, human heart of Jesus, which joins very briefly with the physical human heart of the priest. This grandiose and sublime cosmic event of the Passion of our Lord Jesus takes place during the epiclesis. At the same moment and in unison, the sweet Lamb of God—who is Jesus—is sacrificed by the Eucharistic executing Angels and dies on the altar of the sacrifice of love. From then on, He floods the entire congregation with a supernatural wave of blood and Christic purifying water. These awesome events are brought about by the Holy Spirit—God the Holy Spirit—at the command of God the Almighty Father at the very moment of epiclesis in the Eucharistic liturgy and are proclaimed aloud by the priest celebrant. I love you. I am Saint Padre Pio, and I love you!

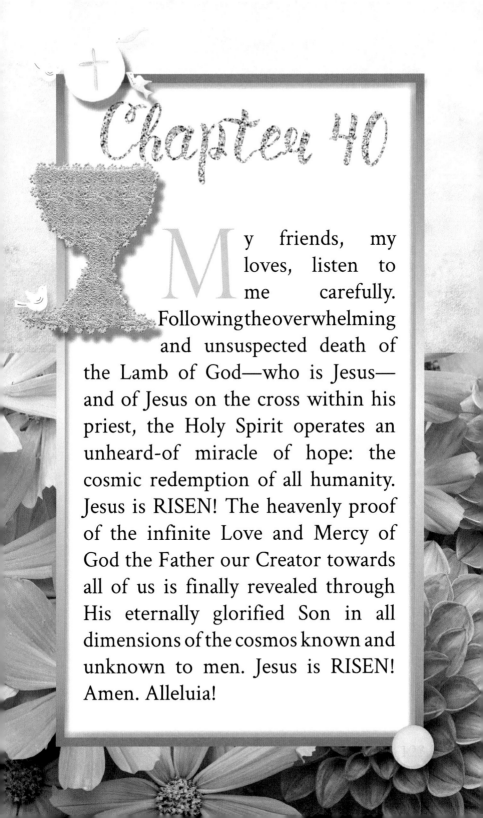

Chapter 40

My friends, my loves, listen to me carefully. Following the overwhelming and unsuspected death of the Lamb of God—who is Jesus—and of Jesus on the cross within his priest, the Holy Spirit operates an unheard-of miracle of hope: the cosmic redemption of all humanity. Jesus is RISEN! The heavenly proof of the infinite Love and Mercy of God the Father our Creator towards all of us is finally revealed through His eternally glorified Son in all dimensions of the cosmos known and unknown to men. Jesus is RISEN! Amen. Alleluia!

Chapter 41

My friends, my loves, listen to me carefully. Today we explore the events following the Paschal Mystery of Jesus's death, which is tirelessly and lovingly repeated at every celebration of the Eucharistic liturgy. Our sweet Jesus, our Lord and our God, resurrects immediately after His painful, although extraordinarily fleeting, death thanks to the operations of the Holy Spirit. What a marvelous miracle of luminous transcendence! What immeasurable cosmic power! What an inestimable treasure of charity and obedience to the Son of Man! I love you. I am Saint Padre Pio, and I love you!

Chapter 42

My friends, my loves in my arms, I love you. It is impossible for me to perfectly illustrate to you the dazzling majesty of our beautiful risen Jesus. At the very moment of His resurrection, Jesus is projected to move from the state of death into life with a prodigiously lightning force that shakes the entirety of Heaven. Our Jesus radiates an inexpressible celestial glory that is eternally sovereign and omnipotent although always fixed on the cross. True, ethereal, and royal grace floats above the consecrated altar, where the consecrated host and the consecrated wine rest. Yes, our Jesus-Love remains on the cross before and after the Eucharistic liturgy by command of God the Father. I love you. I am Saint Padre Pio, and I love you!

Chapter 43

My friends, my loves, listen to me carefully. Why do we see our good Jesus still attached to this infamous cross even after the sacrifice of His Paschal Death? The cross, my loves in my arms, is the very glory of the Son. The cross incorporates all the mysteries of the redemption of all mankind as conceived by God the Father, the Creator and Judge of all. Keep your faith centered on the cross of Jesus and your soul will be routed directly and peacefully onto the Heart of the Father, on Earth as it is in Heaven. Amen. Alleluia!

Chapter 44

My friends, my loves, listen to me carefully. Immediately after the very brief Pascal Death of our beautiful and powerful Jesus, grace itself is risen with a magnificent splendor with no equivalent on Earth. However, the gentle Lamb of God—who is Jesus—whose neck was lacerated during the sacrifice of Love on the altar and whose blood was poured out alongside Christic, purifying water in superabundance on the souls of the congregation, remains in a state of Paschal Death for a slightly longer period. In fact, the duration of the Lamb's death is proportional to the time necessary for the blood and the divine merciful water to carry out the mystical whitening of sins and offenses against God and against men within the affected souls. This process takes place to the extent that the soul is repentant and possesses great faith in God and Jesus. I love you. I am Saint Padre Pio, and I love you!

Beautiful catholic parish
church indoor view of the Virgin Mary, Saint Mary

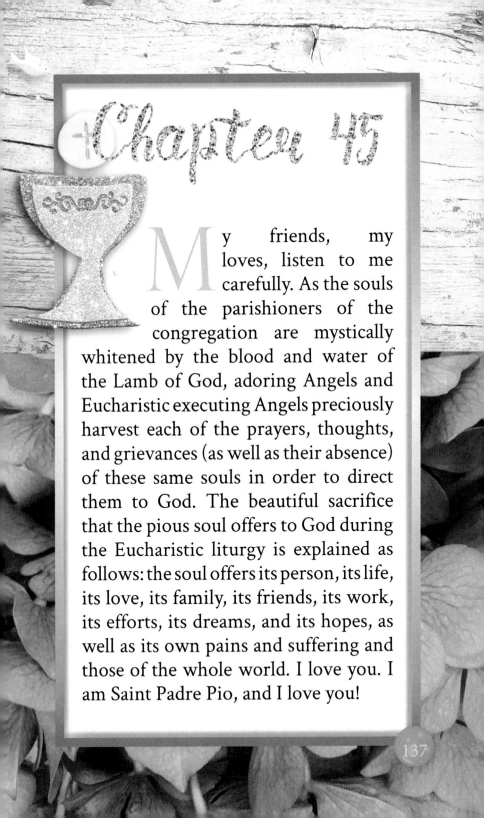

Chapter 45

My friends, my loves, listen to me carefully. As the souls of the parishioners of the congregation are mystically whitened by the blood and water of the Lamb of God, adoring Angels and Eucharistic executing Angels preciously harvest each of the prayers, thoughts, and grievances (as well as their absence) of these same souls in order to direct them to God. The beautiful sacrifice that the pious soul offers to God during the Eucharistic liturgy is explained as follows: the soul offers its person, its life, its love, its family, its friends, its work, its efforts, its dreams, and its hopes, as well as its own pains and suffering and those of the whole world. I love you. I am Saint Padre Pio, and I love you!

Chapter 46

My friends, my loves, listen to me carefully. During the recitation of the Lord's Prayer, which takes place in the last stages of the Eucharistic liturgy, our sweet Lamb of God—who is Jesus—still lies dead on the altar. The Lamb is collected with unimaginable tenderness by the adoring Angels and Eucharistic executors. He is lifted and transported with perfect gentleness and reverence upward to Heaven, to Paradise, to the deepest Heavens, to the Heart of the Father. The angels also carry the sacrifices of the souls present at the liturgy skyward, as you know. During this journey, the angels meticulously and efficiently repair the incision made on Jesus' neck, and His wound heals completely. Our Lamb of Grace is RISEN! Glory to God in the highest Heaven, and peace on Earth to the souls He loves. Amen. Alleluia!

Chapter 47

My friends, my loves, listen to me carefully. The goodness and generosity of Christ Jesus our Savior cannot be understood by human intelligence; however, it is enough for you, dear reader who sees these lines at this moment in the history of your life and of humanity, to know that His Love—the Love of Christ for you—is infinitely great such that you cannot fathom it. The proof of this will be revealed to you in the following pages. I love you. I am Saint Padre Pio, and I love you!

The mystery of the multiplicity and indivisibility of the saints among us is revealed in this book! Glory to God!

≈ Pio

Chapter 48

My friends, my loves, listen to me carefully. Today, I will explain to you the wonderful mystery of the Blessed Sacrament of Communion in the Eucharistic liturgy. As explained at the beginning of this book blessed by God, my love in my arms, a soul which goes to Communion must remain in a state of adoration, reverence, and deep gratitude for this providential gift which is the Life in Jesus. Amen. Alleluia!

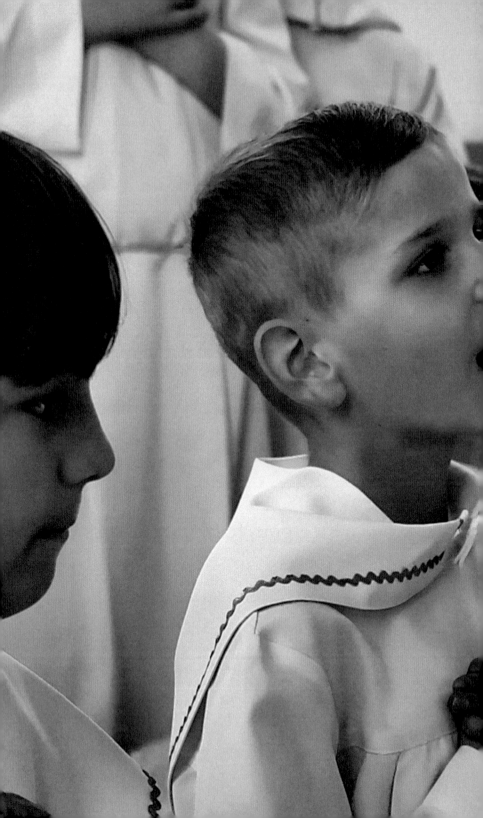

Chapter 49A

My friends, my loves, listen to me carefully. You remember that Jesus our Savior is RISEN after His brief Paschal Death within his Catholic priest and that He floats with magnificent and triumphant luminosity above the altar of the sacrifice of love, where the host and the consecrated wine rest. I have taught you that every consecrated host and every consecrated drop of blood is like a door that opens to infinity— this infinity is the Holy Trinity itself, better known as LOVE. Every soul in harmony and reconciliation with God, its Creator and Judge, who consumes the consecrated host or the consecrated blood receives not only the body, blood, soul, and divinity, of our Lord Jesus, our Savior and our God, but also the past, present, and future of the entire Creation, which was designed by Him, for Him, and through Him, our Lord Jesus Christ. The Eucharist, my loves, is the very life of Jesus and the very life in Jesus.

Chapter 49½

Trembling with joy, I repeat the first lines of this book blessed by God: the Eucharist, my children, is the very life of Paradise, the very life of eternity, the very life of the Kingdom of God! Amen. Alleluia!

Chapter 50

My friends, my loves, listen to me carefully. We are nearing the end of our discussion on the Eucharist—the sublime and gracious consolation of the Father given to humanity by His Son, our Lord and our Redeemer. I want to address the phenomenon of the consumption of the consecrated host and the consecrated blood. When a soul in harmony and reconciliation with God receives Communion, the beneficial and salutary supernatural effects received by the soul, which are necessary for redemption, last much longer than the minimum time it takes for the physical embodiment of Communion to dissolve in the mouth and pass through the gastrointestinal system. Indeed, it is the human soul that receives the life of Jesus and the life in Jesus, not the stomach! Consequently, this perfect nourishment, ecstasy, blessing, transformation, sanctification, and annihilation in Jesus persists for hours, days, weeks, months, and years. I love you. I am Saint Padre Pio, and I love you!

Chapter 51

My friends, my loves, listen to me carefully. The ideal period of fasting preceding the reception of the Sacrament of the Eucharist varies depending on one's health and of the physical body of the soul preparing for the wonderful moment of Communion. Ask the Holy Spirit to reveal to you what you can and cannot tolerate. I love you. I am Saint Padre Pio, and I love you!

I speak to you in all the languages that exist on Earth.

~ Pio

Bulgarian Church of St. Stephen on the shore of the Golden Horn. Known as the Iron Church

Chapter 52

I am a Holy Logos: my mystical presence is experienced and visible within a unique etheric dimension that belongs exclusively to me and that covers the surface of the entire Earth. This is why my presence is continuous and universal in every Catholic Church throughout the world. Glory to God for investing so much power in me, His simple servant! Amen! Alleluia!

Chapter 53

My friends, my loves in my arms, we conclude this brief exposition on the true knowledge of the Sacrament of the Eucharist, the sacrament of sacraments. This holy gift, which originates from the heights of Heaven—the Heart of the Father—is intended for the depths of your heart—the seat of your soul—by virtue of the gift of the physical Heart of Jesus our Redeemer and the heart of his Catholic priest celebrant. Read and frequently reread the teachings revealed here, for God the Almighty Father Himself has allowed you to read this book blessed by Him, the Creator and Judge of all, at this precise moment in your life. May your soul prostrate itself and profess these golden words here and now: Jesus, I love you; God the Father, I love you; Holy Spirit I love you!

I look at you and I love you! I am Saint Padre Pio, and I love you! Amen! Alleluia!

I love you,
~ Pio

Church of St. Mark timelapse and parliament building
Zagreb, Croatia. Top view from Kula
Lotrscak tower viewpoint

Afterword

On the Day of Judgment, the infinite Mercy of God, Abba Father, contained in the books of this collection—and particularly in this book you have just read—will be revealed to you.

May the Glory of God the Father and God the Son flood within you today as you experience new Life in Him, Jesus my Beloved, our Lord and our Savior!

Marie-Josée

About the Author

Marie-Josée Thibault's life is in no way similar to yours. When she wakes, the saints of Heaven visit her, talk to her, teach her, and pray intensely with her. When such mystical sessions draw to a close, she greets with great respect and deep reverence the Masters of the Heavenly Court. This servant of the Lord spends the rest of the day in the company of her guardian angel, who continues her spiritual education and ceaselessly protects her from the perils of this fallen world.

About the Author

Bestowed by the Heavenly Father, her gifts of clairvoyance and clairaudience allow her to remain in continuous contact with the supernatural dimension juxtaposed with ours, where the soul is born of the Spirit through Jesus and Mary. She prays that, one day soon, the entire human race will give glory to the Father, the Son, and the Holy Spirit.

Also by the Author A

- Abba, Your Father, Speaks: Book I
- Abba, Your Father, Speaks: Book II
- Abba, Your Father, Speaks: Book III
- Dear Humanity: Book 1
- Dear Humanity: Book 2
- St Therese of Lisieux Speaks - Book 1: I Am The Heart of the Rose
- Saint Francis of Assisi Speaks - Book 1

Also by the Author B

- Saint Francis of Assisi Speaks - Book 2
- Saint Martin de Porres Speaks - Book 1
- Saint Bernadette Speaks - Book 1
- Saint Joan of Arc Speaks - Book 1
- Saint Padre Pio Speaks: Book 1
- Saint John the Baptist Speaks

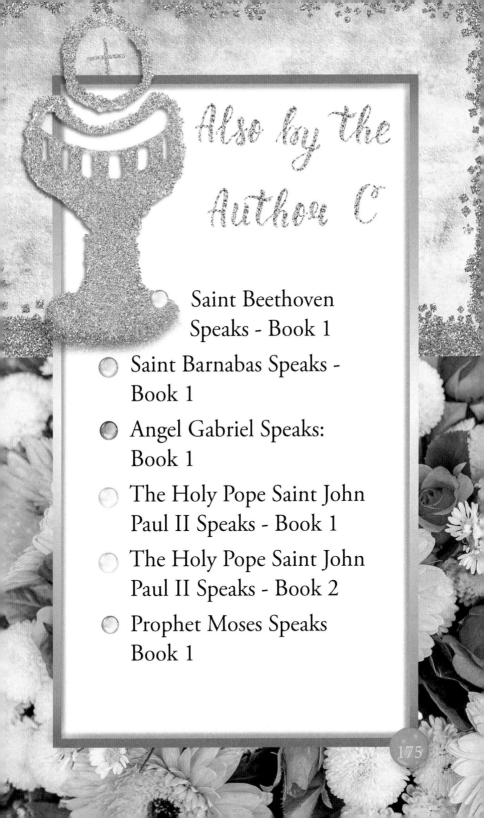

Also by the Author C

Saint Beethoven
Speaks - Book 1

Saint Barnabas Speaks -
Book 1

Angel Gabriel Speaks:
Book 1

The Holy Pope Saint John
Paul II Speaks - Book 1

The Holy Pope Saint John
Paul II Speaks - Book 2

Prophet Moses Speaks
Book 1

Made in the USA
Las Vegas, NV
09 December 2024

13722325R00112